# FUN Sports FOR FITNESS

# CAMPING

Written by

Julie K. Lundgren

Rourke
Educational Media

rourkeeducationalmedia.com

Scan for Related Titles
and Teacher Resources

www.rourkeeducationalmedia.com

PHOTO CREDITS: Photo credits: Cover © Justin Horrocks, elrPhoto; Title Page © MorganL; Page 4 © Paul Moore; Page 5 © PhotoSky 4t com; Page 6 © Pahham; Page 7 © Volkova Anna; Page 8 © Karin Hildebrand Lau; Page 9 © Nathan Doctor; Page 10 © Andrey Kiselev; Page 11 © photo25th, Tatiana Popova, Sony Ho, Marek CECH, maxp; Page 12 © Marc Dietrich, Feng Yu, Darryl Brooks; Page 13 © Robert Churchill; Page 14 © Photographer London; Page 15 © MorganL; Page 16 © Dan Roundhill; Page 17 © CEFutcher, JahartFord; Page 18 © Taily, Miguel Angel Salinas Salinas, Vallentin Vassileff; Page 19 © Indreky; Page 20 © andipantz, SasPartout; Page 21 © Elenathewise, ZTS; Page 22 © Kokhanchikov

Editor: Jill Sherman

Cover Designer: Tara Raymo

Interior Designer: Jen Thomas

**Library of Congress PCN Data**

Camping / Lundgren, Julie K.
Fun Sports for Fitness
   ISBN 978-1-62169-860-9 (hardcover)
   ISBN 978-1-62169-755-8 (softcover)
   ISBN 978-1-62169-962-0 (e-Book)
Library of Congress Control Number:  2013936465

**Also Available as:**

Rourke Educational Media
Printed in the United States of America,
North Mankato, Minnesota

Rourke
Educational Media

rourkeeducationalmedia.com

customerservice@rourkeeducationalmedia.com • PO Box 643328 Vero Beach, Florida 32964

# TABLE OF CONTENTS

# EXPLORING THE GREAT OUTDOORS

People camp for many reasons. Some like to enjoy nature and relax, while others want to test their survival skills or travel. Camping can be as simple as pitching a tent in the backyard or as challenging as two or three weeks in the wilderness.

*Backpacking combines the activities of hiking and camping for an overnight stay in backcountry wilderness.*

Campers learn new skills, go for hikes, and enjoy starry skies. Camping is a good way to learn about the land, plants, and animals in that area. They may spend time with friends, meet new ones, or enjoy the peace and quiet.

One of the first things any camper should learn is how to find the North Star just in case you find yourself in the woods after dark.

The North Star has guided sailors, astronomers, and travelers across the planet for centuries. The North Star, or Polaris, is famous for holding nearly still in our sky while the rest of the northern sky moves around it.

# READY, SET, CAMP!

Camping trips are more fun when everyone helps plan where to go and what activities you will do when you get there. Consider people's abilities and experience. The more wild and distant the location, the greater the skills needed to take care of yourself and others.

State parks often have **campsites** with electricity, running water, flush toilets, and showers. Call ahead to reserve a site in popular campgrounds. Many places allow campers to make reservations up to a year in advance.

*Some campsites are just empty, open spaces with room for a fire and a picnic table.*

Always bring the
right bedding and clothing to stay
warm. Use a plastic ground cloth
under your tent to help keep dry.

Using a list, pack **gear**, clothes, and food that make sense for the season, the length of the trip, and the planned activities. Driving to the campsite allows campers to bring a few extras, while those canoeing or walking should pack only essentials.

Before each trip be sure to clean your equipment. Then set up your tent to check for missing parts or damage. Make repairs to any damaged equipment. Borrow or rent any gear you don't own.

## Basic Camping List

### Sleeping:
- tent and plastic liner
- sleeping bag and pad
- waterproof rain **tarp** and nylon rope

### Personal Items:
- change of clothes, including long pants
- sweater
- jacket or windbreaker
- rain gear, including coat and pants
- sun hat and winter cap
- sturdy shoes
- sunscreen, sunglasses, lip balm
- toothbrush, toothpaste, bar soap, towel
- insect **repellent**
- water bottle and small day pack

### Tools:
- flashlight with fresh batteries
- map and compass
- first aid kit, duct tape, safety pins, and whistle

### Cooking:
- camp stove with fuel, matches
- one or two cooking pots and large spoon
- sharp knife, wrapped or protected
- cup for cold or hot drinks, spoon, and bowl
- wash basin, dish soap, and dish cloth
- container with water

### Fun Extras:
- camera
- journal and pencil
- binoculars and field guides
- swimsuit, card game, or camp chair

Pack enough food for the number of people and the number of days of the trip. Dry food weighs less than canned food and takes up less space.

Trail mix boosts the energy of hungry campers in need of a snack. To make trail mix, combine dried fruits like raisins, apricots, cranberries, or banana chips with dry cereal, candy, and nuts. Beware of adding chocolate chips. They could melt.

**MENU IDEAS INCLUDE:**

noodles, soup mixes

tuna

bagels, pita bread

peanut butter

oatmeal

potatoes

cookies

powdered drinks

NO REFRIGERATION NEEDED

# SETTING UP THE CAMPSITE

Although it is tempting to play and explore when you arrive at your campsite, set up camp while it is still daylight. Most campsites have a flat place for the tent and a **fire ring**. Pitch the tent, find water, and gather firewood, if the park allows it.

Good burning wood must be dry. Test pieces by breaking off a small bit and listening for a crisp snap. Remove old coals, clean off cooking grates, and always have a bucket of water nearby.

# CAMPSITE KITCHEN

**Nutritious** yet simple meals keep everyone fueled for fun. Cooking over a campfire takes patience and skill. Many campers prepare cold meals or use a camp stove for breakfast and lunch, and save the campfire for the evening meal when they have more time. The best cooking fires glow with hot coals, not leaping flames.

## CAMPING TIP

Only prepare the amount of food you think your group can eat. Store leftovers in sealable plastic bags to take home with you. Burning or burying uneaten food attracts bears and other animals. Animals that learn they can find regular meals at campsites become pests, or even dangerous.

S'mores remain a favorite camp dessert. To make s'mores, sandwich a piece of chocolate bar and a hot, roasted marshmallow between two graham crackers.

When camping in bear country, protect food supplies by storing them where bears cannot reach. Sometimes campground managers provide a special metal box at each site for this purpose. Food, drinks, garbage, pet food, toothpaste, and lip balm all attract bears.

Another way to protect food is to hang the food pack from a rope over a tree branch at least ten feet (3 meters) from the ground and the same distance from the tree trunk.

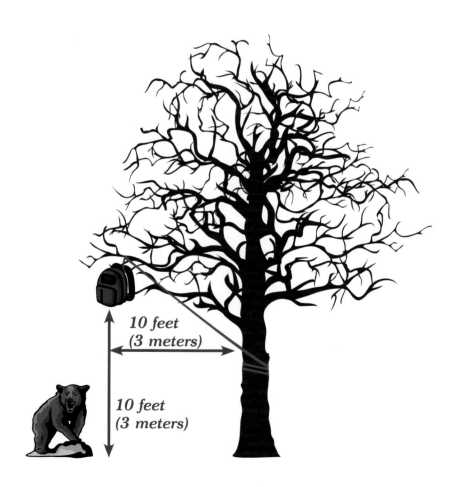

10 feet
(3 meters)

10 feet
(3 meters)

# BE BEAR AWARE

Bears have a knack for sniffing out food. Never store it in the tent. Each evening, clean up your camp to avoid unwanted visitors. If you see a bear, do not feed or approach it. Some campers carry bear spray to use on a bear in case it attacks.

# CAMPING SAFETY

Be prepared for challenges and they will not ruin your fun. Know how to identify plants like poison ivy. Apply insect repellent and cover up with clothing if biting insects get bad. Tuck your pants into your socks to protect against **ticks**. Be sure to check for them daily, especially behind your ears and the back of your head. Prevent sunburn by applying sunscreen several times a day.

*Wash tick bites and apply antibiotic cream. Report any redness around the bite area to your doctor. Ticks can carry disease.*

*Poison ivy can be identified by its shiny green leaves, three per stem.*

Learn how and when to use the items in the first aid kit. Commonly used items include tweezers for tick removal, **calamine lotion** for rashes and bug bites, and bandage strips and antibiotic cream for cuts and scrapes.

Drink plenty of water! Dehydration, a condition caused by not drinking enough water, can sneak up on a busy camper. One of the first symptoms of dehydration is feeling thirsty. More serious symptoms include headaches and vomiting.

Camping and other outdoor activities help people develop an understanding of the natural world and respect for the Earth. As campers gain experience, they also gain confidence in themselves and their abilities. Pitch a tent and get ready for a lifetime of camping fun!

Leave no trace is your wilderness motto. Leave the area and your campsite cleaner than you found it.

# GLOSSARY

**calamine lotion** (KAL-uh-mine LOH-shun): a pinkish liquid that soothes itchy skin

**campsites** (KAMP-sites): places where campers set up their sleeping and eating areas

**fire ring** (FYR RING): a circle of rocks or a thick metal ring surrounding a fire pit, to prevent flames from spreading

**gear** (GIHR): tools or equipment needed for camping, such as a tent and sleeping bag

**nutritious** (noo-TRISH-uhss): healthy food that provides your body with vitamins, minerals, and energy

**repellent** (rih-PELL-uhnt): a spray or cream that causes pests like insects to stay away

**tarp** (TARP): a strong, waterproof sheet or cloth

**ticks** (TICKS): very small creatures that attach themselves to people and animals and drink their blood

# INDEX

# WEBSITES TO VISIT

www.rei.com

www.youthoutdoorsusa.com/kids_camping_websites.htm

www.camping-field-guide.com

# SHOW WHAT YOU KNOW

1. Why is it important to make a camping list before you go on a camping trip?

2. If you don't clean up your food after cooking, what might happen?

3. Can you name some reasons people enjoy camping?

4. How do campers find their way at night?

5. What items should be included in a safety kit?